W9-AYF-126

SCHOLASTIC

Instant Practice Packets
Alphabet

Joan Novelli & Holly Grundon

New York • Toronto • London • Auckland • Sydney
Mexico City • New Delhi • Hong Kong • Buenos Aires

Teaching *Resources*

Scholastic Inc. grants teachers permission to photocopy the reproducible pages in this book for classroom use. No other part of this publication may be reproduced in whole or in part, or stored in a retrieval system, or transmitted in any form or by any means, electronic, photocopying, recording, or otherwise, without written permission of the publisher. For information regarding permission, write to Scholastic Inc., 557 Broadway, New York, NY 10012-3999.

Edited by Immacula A. Rhodes
Cover design by Wendy Chan
Interior design by Joan Novelli and Holly Grundon
Interior illustrations by Teresa Anderko, Maxie Chambliss, Dave Clegg, and Rusty Fletcher

Photograph, page 4, copyright © 2011 by Joan Novelli. Used by permission.
Interior design and text copyright © 2011 by Joan Novelli and Holly Grundon.
Illustrations copyright © 2011 by Scholastic Inc.

ISBN: 978-0-545-30586-0

Published by Scholastic Inc.
All rights reserved.
Printed in the U.S.A.

5 6 7 8 9 10   40   18 17 16 15 14 13

Contents

Introduction 4

Teaching With the Alphabet Packets 5

Using the Supplemental Reproducible Activity Pages . . . 7

Connections to the Standards 10

References & Resources 10

Alphabet Packets

Letter	Page	Letter	Page
Aa 11		Nn 63	
Bb 15		Oo 67	
Cc 19		Pp 71	
Dd 23		Qq 75	
Ee 27		Rr 79	
Ff 31		Ss 83	
Gg 35		Tt 87	
Hh 39		Uu 91	
Ii 43		Vv 95	
Jj 47		Ww 99	
Kk 51		Xx 103	
Ll 55		Yy 107	
Mm 59		Zz 111	

Supplemental Reproducible Activity Pages

Letter Formation Practice Template 115

Letter Cards 116

Alphabet Mini-Book 120

Missing Letters Game 123

Alphabet Hand Signs Mini-Poster 128

Introduction

When five-year old Luisa writes her name, she proudly announces each letter in turn and carefully adds a curlicue for good measure. "It's cursive," she explains. Luisa recognizes that these lines and shapes are something special and delights in her growing knowledge of the alphabet. As Luisa continues to learn about letters, she will develop the alphabet recognition skills that are essential for learning to read. Luisa is happily on her way to becoming a reader and building a strong foundation that predicts future school success.

Alphabet recognition—knowing the names for letters and the sounds they represent—begins for many young children with the familiar song, "A, B, C, D, E, F, G... ." As children sing the alphabet song again and again, they learn the letter names, an important first step for alphabet recognition. But children also need to learn the printed form of each letter (uppercase and lowercase, in and out of sequence) and the most frequent sound each letter represents. Research shows that speed and accuracy are two important factors in alphabet recognition. Children who can recognize letters with speed and accuracy can more efficiently focus on sound-letter relationships as they learn to read (Adams, 1990; as cited in Blevins, 2006). Over-learning the letters—their names, shapes, and sounds—is recommended for achieving this goal.

Instant Practice Packets: Alphabet provides the repeated practice children need to thoroughly learn the letters of the alphabet. These ready-to-go, reproducible packets—one for each letter—are designed to help children build a foundation for early reading success. The format and sequence of activities on the pages support children in working independently.

TEACHING TIP

Pages 1 and 2 of each packet feature letter-formation practice. For children who are left-handed, consider writing the target letter at the end (right side) of each practice line to provide a model they can easily see as they trace and write the letters.

Instant Practice Packets: Alphabet • © 2011 by Joan Novelli & Holly Grundon • Scholastic Teaching Resources

In addition to letter recognition activities, opportunities to practice letter formation are an important component of each packet. In writing letters of the alphabet, children begin to notice the different features of letters (such as height, straight and curved lines, intersecting lines, and loops), which "significantly helps letter recognition" (Clay, 2002, 2006). From tracing and writing letters to turning them into works of art, letter formation activities are built into each page. Additional highlights for each packet include:

- multisensory activities that reflect research about the way young children learn—for example, the hand-sign component of each packet adds a kinesthetic connection

- activities that provide necessary practice with letter recognition in isolation as well as in the context of words

- key pictures and words that help children learn letter-sound relationships

- predictable text that features each target letter to help children take the next step in becoming readers

- kid-friendly layouts that keep interest high

TEACHING TIP

Research shows that "supporting literacy and language skills in the first language provides a base for successful literacy development in the second language" (Snow, Burns, & Griffin, 1998, as cited by Northwest Regional Educational Laboratory, 2005). One way to implement that strategy using the packets is to give English Language Learners opportunities to teach others how to say the letter names and words for pictures in their first language.

Teaching With the Alphabet Packets

The packets in this book are organized in alphabetical order, but can be used in any sequence to meet your instructional needs. To prepare the packets for use, photocopy the pages and staple to bind. Introduce the packets by "walking" through each page with children. Review each activity and model how to complete it. The packets allow children to work at their own pace, and taking time in advance to review directions will facilitate their independence. Following is an overview of each page.

PAGE 1: The first page of each packet introduces the target letter and provides guided practice with letter formation. In addition, children explore different letter styles (through a variety of fonts) and take a turn creating a letter style all their own! (Encourage creativity as children

TEACHING TIP

Instant Practice Packets: Alphabet offers effective support for Response to Intervention (RTI). For example, children who do not have adequate knowledge of the alphabet and therefore struggle academically with reading may benefit from the systematic approach the packets provide—from letter-writing practice that draws attention to important features of each letter to picture-word combinations that reinforce letter-sound relationships. Additionally, the formatted practice pages make it easy for these learners to focus on specific skills.

"design" a new way to write the letter.) They also learn that hand signs are another way to form letters and can practice making the hand sign for the target letter. This kinesthetic component helps further reinforce children's letter learning experiences.

PAGE 2: The top section of this page gives children continued practice in letter-writing. At the bottom, children take a "Letter Walk," which engages them in noticing similarities and differences among letters as they identify uppercase and lowercase examples of the target letter along a path.

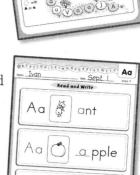

PAGE 3: With an alphabet-book-like setup, this page features pictures and words that help children learn the sound commonly associated with the target letter. Children trace the letter and write it to complete the word for each picture. To reinforce sound-letter relationships, encourage children to say the name for each letter as they trace or write it and the word for the picture. In the final section on this page, children draw their own picture to represent the letter and write (or dictate) the word. Note: *In the case of the letter* x, *the pictures on page 3 illustrate words in which* x *appears as a final consonant.* (*Words with* x *at the beginning are generally too advanced for this purpose.*)

PAGE 4: "Star Words" introduces children to words that begin with (or end with, in the case of the letter *x*) the target letter, including many from sight-word vocabulary lists (such as Dolch and Fry). Children trace the letters to spell four words, then color the stars to show which of those words they can read. As an extension, you might build a wall chart of the Star Words from each packet. To use the chart, point out and read the words with children frequently to support acquisition of sight-word vocabulary. Other features on this page include "Animal ABCs" and "doodle." With Animal ABCs, children practice writing the target letter to complete the name of an animal. The predictable text in this activity encourages early reading skills. The doodle activity invites children to form the letter, then have fun transforming it into a picture. This exercise encourages a playfulness that motivates further learning.

Using the Supplemental Reproducible Activity Pages

The supplemental activities (pages 115–128) are designed to provide the repetition children need to strengthen alphabet recognition skills. A review of these pages, along with suggestions for teaching with the activities, follows.

Letter Formation Practice Template (page 115)

Customize this page to provide additional letter-writing practice for up to five different letters. First, photocopy the page and write the target letter at the beginning of the line to provide a model for children. Then make copies for children to complete.

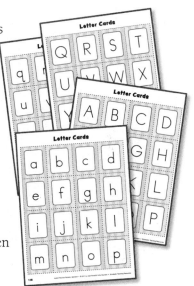

• •

Letter Cards (pages 116–119)

Copy and laminate sets of these uppercase and lowercase letter cards for an endless variety of activities that will actively engage children in learning the alphabet. Suggestions follow.

Letter Buddies: Copy the uppercase letter cards; leave the page intact. Copy the lowercase letter cards and cut them apart. Mix up the lowercase letters and have children match each card to the corresponding uppercase letter. Alternately, have children match the uppercase letter cards to an intact page of lowercase letters.

Big and Little Letter Match: Have children use the cards to play Concentration. Pre-select and cut out a set of 8–10 uppercase and lowercase letter pairs for children to match in the game. (Using the entire set of cards may be too challenging for some children.)

Alphabet Soup: Copy and cut apart a set of uppercase and lowercase letter cards. Label two paper bowls (on the inside) "BIG LETTERS" and "little letters." Write a few uppercase and lowercase letters on each bowl to provide visual support. Mix up the uppercase and lowercase letter cards and have children sort them into the corresponding bowls.

Letter Line Up: Provide either a set of uppercase or lowercase letter cards. Mix up the cards and have children line them up in alphabetical order. Children can work with a partner, taking turns to find each letter. If they like, they can use a one-minute (or more) timer and see how many cards they can place in alphabetical order before time runs out (and with continued practice, notice how that number grows). Encourage children to sing the alphabet song as they work to help figure out which letter comes next.

Before and After: Copy two sets of cards (either uppercase or lowercase), each on a different color paper. Spread out one set of cards faceup on a table. Shuffle the second set and stack the cards facedown. Have children take turns selecting the top card from the stack, placing it faceup, naming the letter, then searching the cards that are spread out to find the letter that comes before and the letter that comes after it. (For *A* and *Z*, children can find the two letters that come immediately after or before). When finished, children return the "before and after" cards to the table and place the card from the stack to the side.

. . . .

Alphabet Mini-Book (pages 120-122)

This interactive mini-book is designed to extend learning for each packet. To prepare the mini-book, write the target letter in the box provided on the cover and on pages 1–3 before making copies for children. Cut apart the mini-book pages and arrange them in order, then staple to bind. Suggestions for teaching with each page follow.

COVER: Have children write their name in the space at the bottom, then color the picture if they wish.

PAGE 1: This page provides letter formation practice. Write tracing letters as needed at the beginning of each practice line. Give children a star sticker (or stamp) to place next to their best letter.

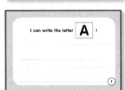

PAGE 2: This activity helps children learn to recognize letters that appear in different fonts, sizes, and colors. To complete the page, have children search for examples of the target letter in magazines, newspapers, and old workbook pages. Have them cut out the letters and glue them in the box to create a letter collage.

PAGE 3: Have children write a large version of the letter in the center of the big box. Model how to trace the letter in one color, then write the letter again with three more colors, each time tracing closely around the outside of the previous color to create a "rainbow."

Instant Practice Packets: Alphabet • © 2011 by Joan Novelli & Holly Grundon • Scholastic Teaching Resources

PAGE 4: The activity on this page strengthens alphabet and sequencing skills. To prepare, write the target letter in one of the four boxes, keeping in mind that children will fill in the letters that come just before and/or after. For example, if the target letter is *A*, write the letter *A* in the first box. Children will then write the next three letters. If the target letter is *Z*, write that letter in the last box so that children can fill in the preceding three letters. You can write target letters such as *D*, *E*, and *F* in any of the boxes since there are at least three letters before and after that children can fill in. [Note: You might program this page before making copies for children.]

PAGE 5: This activity helps children make a connection between letters and words, as they hunt for words that contain the target letter and copy them onto the page. After children complete their mini-books, read the words on this page together to reinforce sound-letter associations.

• •

Missing Letters Game (pages 123–127)

This write-and-erase game provides the repetition children need to learn to recognize and write the letters of the alphabet. Two versions of the game board offer practice separately for both uppercase and lowercase letter forms. Children may play the game independently, with a partner, or with a small group (up to four players). Follow the steps outlined below to prepare the game for use. (For materials and directions for play, see page 125.)

1. Copy the game boards on pages 123 and 124 (enlarge first if desired). Color each game board for added visual appeal, then laminate.

2. Make multiple copies of the game directions, game cards, and the blank game card template (pages 125–127). Laminate the directions and at least four game cards for each game set. (Each player needs a game card, but the cards do not have to be different.) Use the game card template to create new game cards as desired.

3. When not in use, store materials for each game set in a large resealable bag.

• •

Alphabet Hand Signs Mini-Poster (page 128)

This reproducible mini-poster revisits the hand signs featured in each packet to provide children with a complete set of the alphabet. Children can practice each hand sign in turn as they sing the alphabet song and use the hand signs to finger spell familiar words, such as their names. Display the mini-poster in the classroom or make an individual copy for each child.

Connections to the Standards

The activities in this book are designed to support you in meeting the following standards, as outlined by Mid-continent Research for Education and Learning (McREL), an organization that collects and synthesizes national and state curriculum standards—and proposes what teachers should provide for their students to become proficient in language arts, among other curriculum areas.

Common Core State Standards

The activities in this book also correlate with the English Language Arts standards recommended by the Common Core State Standards Initiative, a state-led effort to establish a single set of clear educational standards whose aim is to provide students with a high-quality education. At the time this book went to press, these standards were still being finalized. To learn more, go to www.corestandards.org.

Uses the general skills and strategies of the reading process

- Knows that print and written symbols convey meaning and represent spoken language
- Understands the differences between letters, numbers, and words and knows the significance of spaces between words
- Understands that illustrations and pictures convey meaning
- Knows that print is read from left to right, top to bottom, and that books are read front to back
- Understands level-appropriate sight words and vocabulary (e.g., words for persons, places, things, actions, and feelings; words that appeal to the senses; high-frequency words such as *said*, *was*, and *where*)
- Knows uppercase and lowercase letters of the alphabet and their associated sounds

Uses the general skills and strategies of the writing process

- Knows that writing, including pictures, letters, and words, communicates meaning and information
- Uses knowledge of letters to write or copy familiar words
- Uses writing tools and materials, such as pencils and crayons

Source: Kendall, J. S., & Marzano, R. J. (2004). *Content knowledge: A compendium of standards and benchmarks for K–12 education.* Aurora, CO: Mid-continent Research for Education and Learning. Online database: http://www.mcrel.org/standards-benchmarks/

References & Resources

Blevins, W. (2006). *Phonics from A to Z* (2nd ed.). New York: Scholastic.

Clay, M. M. (2002, 2006). *An observation survey of early literacy achievement* (2nd ed.). Portsmouth, NH: Heinemann.

Northwest Regional Educational Laboratory (2005). "Focus on effectiveness." Retrieved January 10, 2011 from <http://www.netc.org>.

Name: _____ Date: _____ page 1

Write the letter **Aa**.

The letter **A** can look like this.   Make a new **A**.

A	A	A	

The letter **a** can look like this.   Make a new **a**.

a	a	*a*	

Sign It!

You can use hand shapes to make letters. Try making an **Aa**!

Instant Practice Packets: Alphabet • © 2011 by Joan Novelli & Holly Grundon • Scholastic Teaching Resources

Aa

Name: _Kyle_   Date: _____   page 2

Write the letter **Aa**.

A A A A

a a a a

Letter Walk

Take a
Letter Walk.
Color each
◯ with
A or **a**.

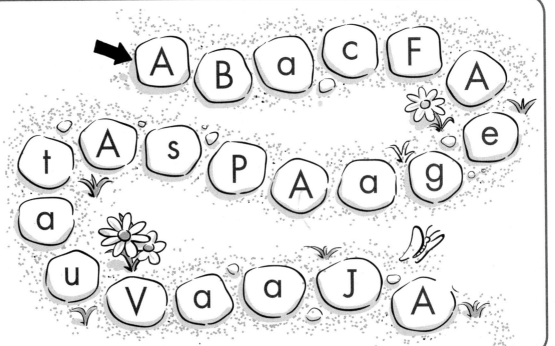

A B a c F A

t A s P A a g e

a

u V a a J A

---

12   *Instant Practice Packets: Alphabet* • © 2011 by Joan Novelli & Holly Grundon • Scholastic Teaching Resources

Name: _Kyle_   Date: _____   page 3

Read and Write

A a   ant

A a   ___pple

A a   cat

Animal

Instant Practice Packets: Alphabet • © 2011 by Joan Novelli & Holly Grundon • Scholastic Teaching Resources

 **Star Words**

Write words with the letter **a**.
Color the ☆ for each word you know.

 am

 an

 and

 at

Animal ABCs

What am I? Write the letter **a** to spell my name.

I am an
_a_lligator!

doodle

Trace the letter **a**.
Turn it into a picture!

Instant Practice Packets: Alphabet • © 2011 by Joan Novelli & Holly Grundon • Scholastic Teaching Resources

Write the letter **Bb**.

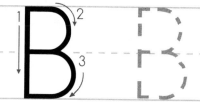

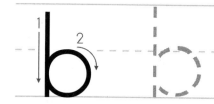

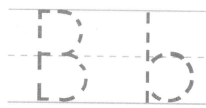

The letter **B** can look like this.   Make a new **B**.

B	B	B	

The letter **b** can look like this.   Make a new **b**.

b	b	b	

Sign It!

You can use hand shapes to make letters. Try making a **Bb**!

Instant Practice Packets: Alphabet • © 2011 by Joan Novelli & Holly Grundon • Scholastic Teaching Resources

Name: _____ Date: _____

Write the letter **Bb**.

B B

b b

Letter Walk

Take a Letter Walk. Color each ◯ with **B** or **b**.

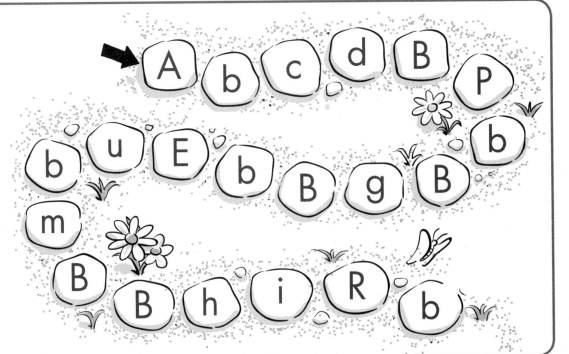

Instant Practice Packets: Alphabet • © 2011 by Joan Novelli & Holly Grundon • Scholastic Teaching Resources

Read and Write

B b  **barn**

B b  ____ **us**

B b _____

 **Star Words**

Write words with the letter **b**.
Color the ☆ for each word you know.

 ☆ be

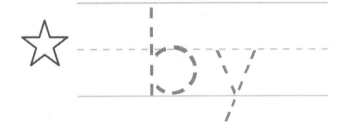 ☆ best

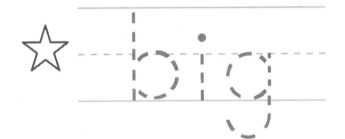 ☆ big

☆ by

 **Animal ABCs**

What am I? Write the letter **b** to spell my name.

I am a ___utterfly!

 **doodle**

Trace the letter **b**.
Turn it into a picture!

Instant Practice Packets: Alphabet • © 2011 by Joan Novelli & Holly Grundon • Scholastic Teaching Resources

Write the letter **Cc**.

C

C

The letter **C** can look like this. Make a new **C**.

C C C

The letter **c** can look like this. Make a new **c**.

c c c

Sign It!

You can use hand shapes to make letters. Try making a **Cc**!

Name: _____ Date: _____

Write the letter **Cc**.

C

C

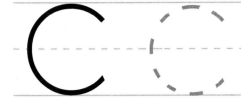

Take a
Letter Walk.
Color each
⬡ with
C or **c**.

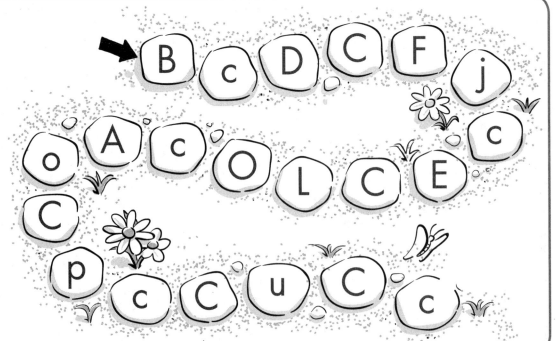

Instant Practice Packets: Alphabet • © 2011 by Joan Novelli & Holly Grundon • Scholastic Teaching Resources

Name: _____ Date: _____

Read and Write

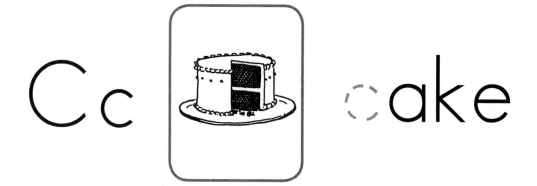

C c   ⟨cake image⟩   ◦ake

◦ ◦   ⟨cat image⟩   ___at

◦ ◦   ⟨blank box⟩   _____

Write words with the letter **c**.
Color the ☆ for each word you know.

☆

☆

☆

☆

Animal ABCs

What am I? Write the
letter **c** to spell my name.

I am a

____ow!

doodle

Trace the letter **c**.
Turn it into a picture!

Instant Practice Packets: Alphabet • © 2011 by Joan Novelli & Holly Grundon • Scholastic Teaching Resources

Write the letter **Dd**.

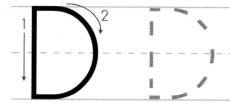

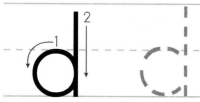

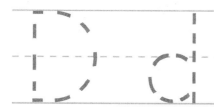

The letter **D** can look like this. Make a new **D**.

D D D

The letter **d** can look like this. Make a new **d**.

d d d

Sign It!

You can use hand shapes to make letters. Try making a **Dd**!

Name: _____ Date: _____

Write the letter **Dd**.

D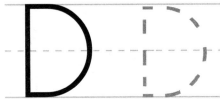

d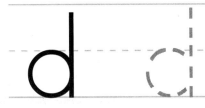

Letter Walk

Take a Letter Walk. Color each ⬭ with **D** or **d**.

D d z D L d

D b W D I B d I

u

E d o d D g

Instant Practice Packets: Alphabet • © 2011 by Joan Novelli & Holly Grundon • Scholastic Teaching Resources

Read and Write

Dd   door

Dd   ___uck

Dd   _____

 **Star Words**

Write words with the letter **d**.
Color the ☆ for each word you know.

☆

☆

☆

☆

Animal ABCs

What am I? Write the letter **d** to spell my name.

I am a

___ og!

Trace the letter **d**.
Turn it into a picture!

doodle

Instant Practice Packets: Alphabet • © 2011 by Joan Novelli & Holly Grundon • Scholastic Teaching Resources

Name: _____ Date: _____ page 1

Write the letter **Ee**.

The letter **E** can look like this.   Make a new **E**.

E	E	E	

The letter **e** can look like this.   Make a new **e**.

e	e	e	

Sign It!

You can use hand shapes to make letters. Try making an **Ee**!

A B C D E F G H I J K L M N O P Q R S T U V W X Y Z

Ee

Name: _____ Date: _____

Write the letter **Ee**.

E E

e e

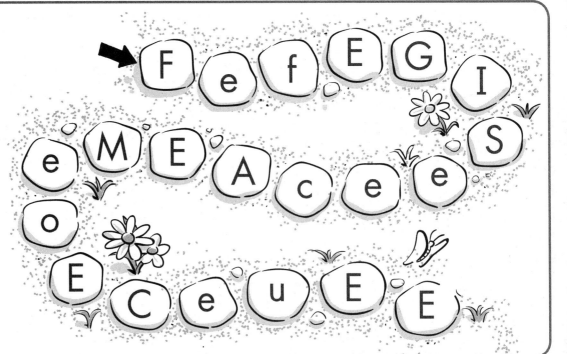

Letter Walk

Take a Letter Walk. Color each ◯ with **E** or **e**.

F e f E G I
e M E A c e e S
o E C e u E E
C

Instant Practice Packets: Alphabet • © 2011 by Joan Novelli & Holly Grundon • Scholastic Teaching Resources

Read and Write

E e   ⊙ ar

E e   ___ gg

E e   _____

Instant Practice Packets: Alphabet • © 2011 by Joan Novelli & Holly Grundon • Scholastic Teaching Resources

Star Words

Write words with the letter **e**.
Color the ☆ for each word you know.

☆ each

☆ eat

☆ eight

☆ even

Animal ABCs

What am I? Write the letter **e** to spell my name.

I am an ___lephant!

doodle

Trace the letter **e**. Turn it into a picture!

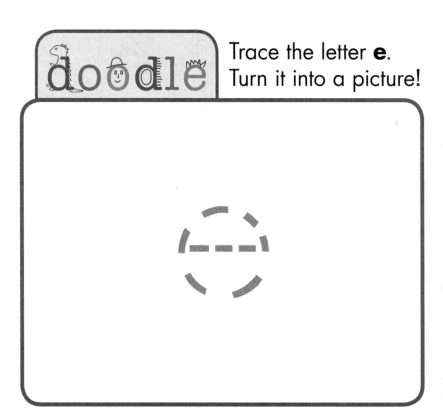

Instant Practice Packets: Alphabet • © 2011 by Joan Novelli & Holly Grundon • Scholastic Teaching Resources

Name: _____ Date: _____ page 1

Write the letter **Ff**.

The letter **F** can look like this.   Make a new **F**.

F	F	F	

The letter **f** can look like this.   Make a new **f**.

f	f	f	

Sign It!

You can use hand shapes to make letters. Try making an **Ff**!

Name: _____ Date: _____ page 2

Write the letter **Ff**.

F

f

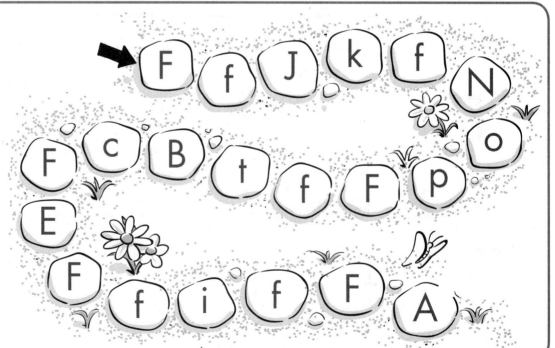

Letter Walk

Take a Letter Walk. Color each ⬡ with **F** or **f**.

Instant Practice Packets: Alphabet • © 2011 by Joan Novelli & Holly Grundon • Scholastic Teaching Resources

Read and Write

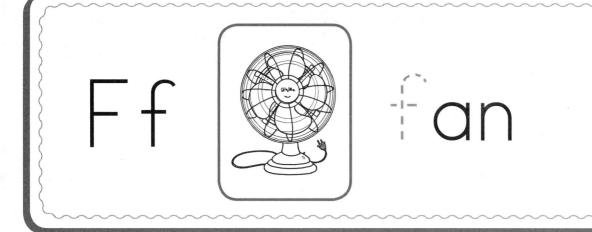

F f   fan

F f   5   ___ive

F f   _____

Star Words

Write words with the letter **f**.
Color the ☆ for each word you know.

☆

☆

☆

☆

Animal ABCs

What am I? Write the
letter **f** to spell my name.

I am a
___ ish!

Trace the letter **f**.
Turn it into a picture!

doodle

Instant Practice Packets: Alphabet • © 2011 by Joan Novelli & Holly Grundon • Scholastic Teaching Resources

Name: _____ Date: _____

Write the letter **Gg**.

The letter **G** can look like this. Make a new **G**.

G	G	G	

The letter **g** can look like this. Make a new **g**.

g	g	g	

Sign It!

You can use hand shapes to make letters. Try making a **Gg**!

Write the letter **Gg**.

G

g

Take a Letter Walk.
Color each ◯ with **G** or **g**.

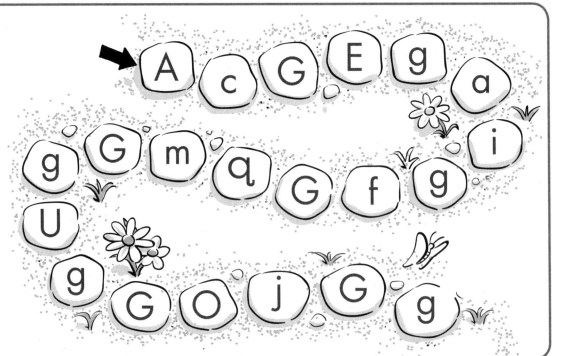

Instant Practice Packets: Alphabet • © 2011 by Joan Novelli & Holly Grundon • Scholastic Teaching Resources

Name: _____ Date: _____

Read and Write

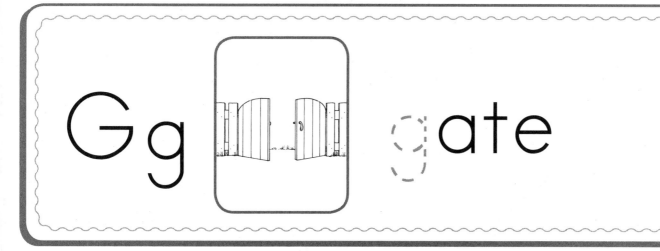

G g   gate

___irl

_____

Instant Practice Packets: Alphabet • © 2011 by Joan Novelli & Holly Grundon • Scholastic Teaching Resources

 **Star Words**

Write words with the letter **g**.
Color the ☆ for each word you know.

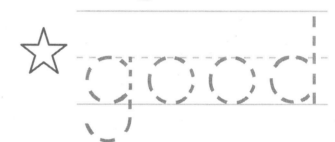

Animal ABCs

What am I? Write the letter **g** to spell my name.

Trace the letter **g**.
Turn it into a picture!

doodle

I am a
____ oat!

Instant Practice Packets: Alphabet • © 2011 by Joan Novelli & Holly Grundon • Scholastic Teaching Resources

Write the letter **Hh**.

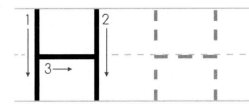

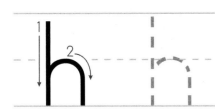

The letter **H** can look like this.   Make a new **H**.

H	H̶	*H*	

The letter **h** can look like this.   Make a new **h**.

h	h	*h*	

Sign It!

You can use hand shapes to make letters. Try making an **Hh**!

Name: _____ Date: _____ page 2

Write the letter **Hh**.

H

h

Take a
Letter Walk.
Color each
◯ with
H or **h**.

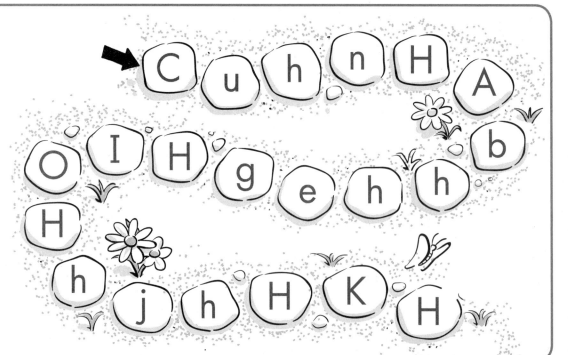

Instant Practice Packets: Alphabet • © 2011 by Joan Novelli & Holly Grundon • Scholastic Teaching Resources

Read and Write

H h  h at

H h  ___ ouse

H h

_____

Star Words

Write words with the letter **h**.
Color the ☆ for each word you know.

☆  has

☆ help

☆  not

☆ how

Animal ABCs

What am I? Write the
letter **h** to spell my name.

I am a

___ orse!

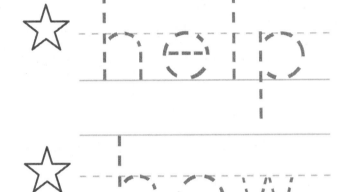
doodle

Trace the letter **h**.
Turn it into a picture!

h

Instant Practice Packets: Alphabet • © 2011 by Joan Novelli & Holly Grundon • Scholastic Teaching Resources

Name: _____   Date: _____   page 1

Write the letter **Ii**.

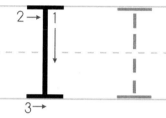

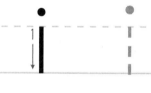

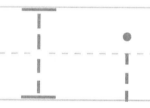

The letter **I** can look like this.   Make a new **I**.

I	l	*I*	

The letter **i** can look like this.   Make a new **i**.

i	i	*i*	

Sign It!

You can use hand shapes to make letters. Try making an **Ii**!

Instant Practice Packets: Alphabet • © 2011 by Joan Novelli & Holly Grundon • Scholastic Teaching Resources

Name: _____ Date: _____

Write the letter **Ii**.

I

i

Letter Walk 👣

Take a Letter Walk. Color each ⬭ with **I** or **i**.

Instant Practice Packets: Alphabet • © 2011 by Joan Novelli & Holly Grundon • Scholastic Teaching Resources

Read and Write

Ii  igloo

I i 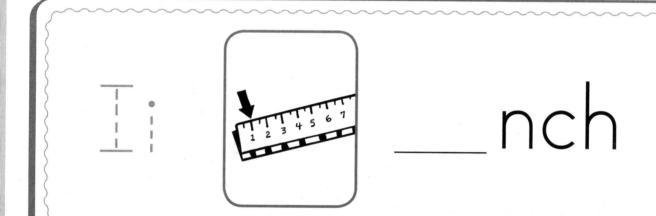 ___nch

I i 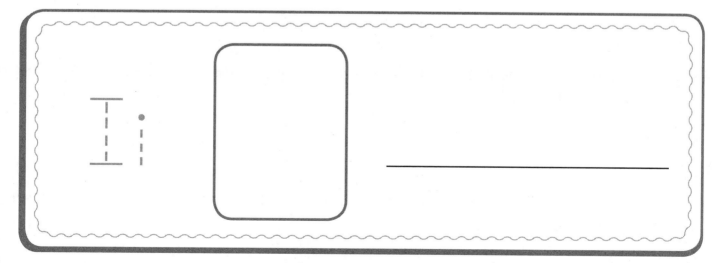 _____

Star Words

Write words with the letter **i**.
Color the ☆ for each word you know.

☆

☆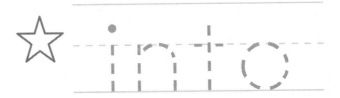

☆ if

☆ it

Animal ABCs

What am I? Write the letter **i** to spell my name.

I am an ___ guana!

doodle

Trace the letter **i**.
Turn it into a picture!

i

Instant Practice Packets: Alphabet • © 2011 by Joan Novelli & Holly Grundon • Scholastic Teaching Resources

Write the letter **Jj**.

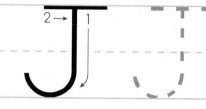

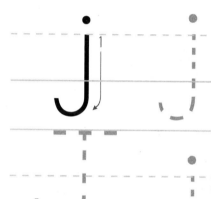

The letter **J** can look like this.   Make a new **J**.

J	J	J	

The letter **j** can look like this.   Make a new **j**.

j	j	j	

Sign It!

You can use hand
shapes to make letters.
Try making a **Jj**!

Name: _____   Date: _____

Write the letter **Jj**.

J J

j j

Letter Walk

Take a
Letter Walk.
Color each
⬭ with
J or **j**.

Instant Practice Packets: Alphabet • © 2011 by Joan Novelli & Holly Grundon • Scholastic Teaching Resources

Read and Write

J j   jam

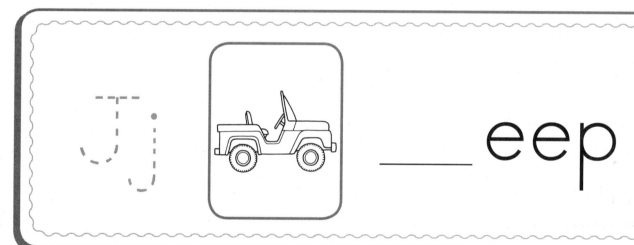

J j   ___ eep

J j   _____

Star Words

Write words with the letter **j**.
Color the ☆ for each word you know.

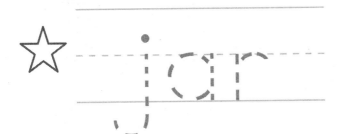

☆ jar

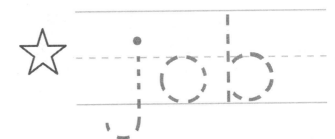

☆ job

☆ jump

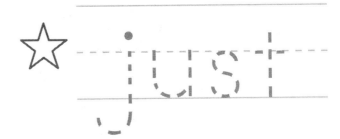

☆ just

Animal ABCs

What am I? Write the
letter **j** to spell my name.

I am a
___ ellyfish!

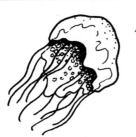

doodle

Trace the letter **j**.
Turn it into a picture!

j

Instant Practice Packets: Alphabet • © 2011 by Joan Novelli & Holly Grundon • Scholastic Teaching Resources

Write the letter **Kk**.

The letter **K** can look like this.   Make a new **K**.

K	K	K	

The letter **k** can look like this.   Make a new **k**.

k	k	k	

Sign It!

You can use hand shapes to make letters. Try making a **Kk**!

Instant Practice Packets: Alphabet • © 2011 by Joan Novelli & Holly Grundon • Scholastic Teaching Resources

Name: _____ Date: _____

Write the letter **Kk**.

K

k

Take a
Letter Walk.
Color each
◯ with
K or **k**.

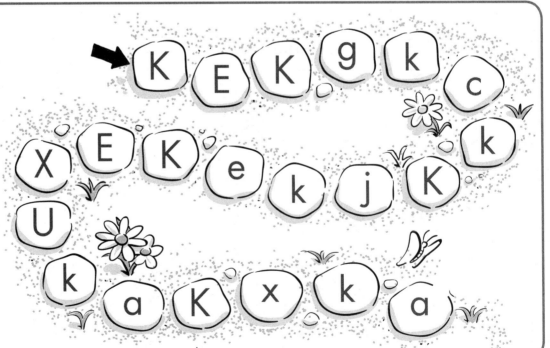

Instant Practice Packets: Alphabet • © 2011 by Joan Novelli & Holly Grundon • Scholastic Teaching Resources

Read and Write

K k   key

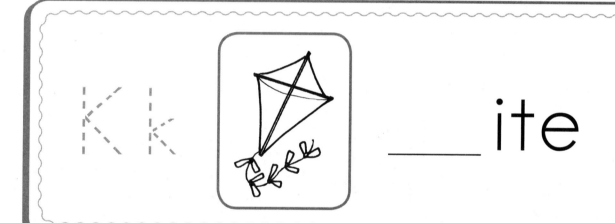

K k   ___ite

K k   _____

Star Words

Write words with the letter **k**.
Color the ☆ for each word you know.

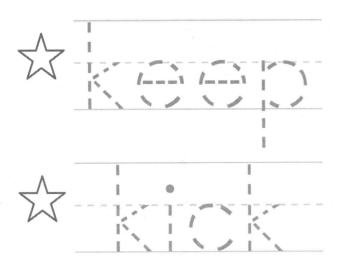

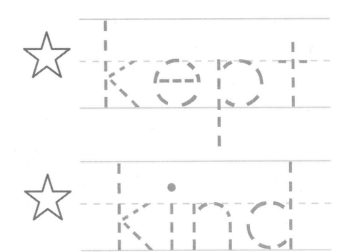

☆ keep   ☆ kept

☆ kick   ☆ kind

Animal ABCs

What am I? Write the
letter **k** to spell my name.

I am a

___ angaroo!

doodle

Trace the letter **k**.
Turn it into a picture!

k

Instant Practice Packets: Alphabet • © 2011 by Joan Novelli & Holly Grundon • Scholastic Teaching Resources

Name: _____ Date: _____ page 1

Write the letter **Ll**.

1 ↓ L
2→

1 ↓ l

The letter **L** can look like this. Make a new **L**.

L	L	L	

The letter **l** can look like this. Make a new **l**.

l	l	l	

Sign It!

You can use hand shapes to make letters. Try making an **Ll**!

Name: _____ Date: _____

Write the letter **Ll**.

Letter Walk

Take a
Letter Walk.
Color each
◯ with
L or **l**.

Instant Practice Packets: Alphabet • © 2011 by Joan Novelli & Holly Grundon • Scholastic Teaching Resources

Read and Write

L l 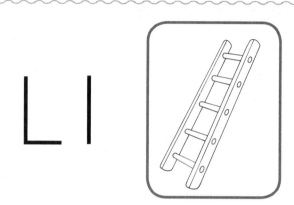 ¦adder

L l 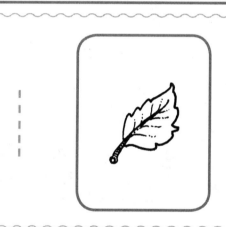 ___eaf

L l

_____

Write words with the letter **l**.
Color the ☆ for each word you know.

☆

☆

☆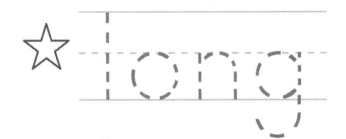

☆

Animal ABCs

What am I? Write the letter **l** to spell my name.

I am a

____ eopard!

doodle

Trace the letter **l**.
Turn it into a picture!

Instant Practice Packets: Alphabet • © 2011 by Joan Novelli & Holly Grundon • Scholastic Teaching Resources

Name: _____ Date: _____

Write the letter **Mm**.

The letter **M** can look like this.   Make a new **M**.

M	M	M	

The letter **m** can look like this.   Make a new **m**.

m	m	m	

Sign It!

You can use hand shapes to make letters. Try making an **Mm**!

Name: _____ Date: _____

Write the letter **Mm**.

Letter Walk 👣

Take a Letter Walk. Color each ⬡ with **M** or **m**.

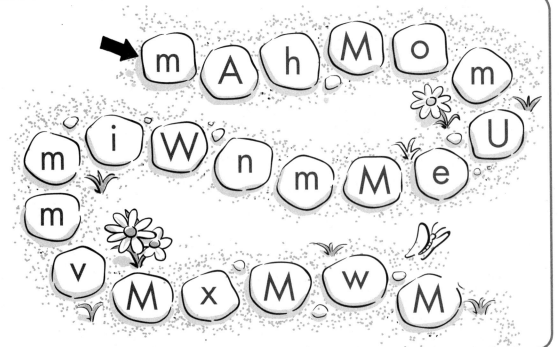

Instant Practice Packets: Alphabet • © 2011 by Joan Novelli & Holly Grundon • Scholastic Teaching Resources

Read and Write

M m   mice

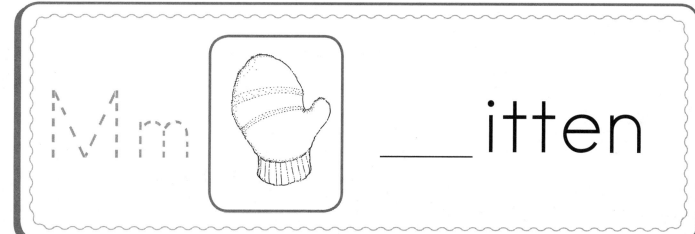

M m   ___itten

M m   _____

Star Words

Write words with the letter **m**.
Color the ☆ for each word you know.

☆  make

☆  many

☆  me

☆  my

Animal ABCs

What am I? Write the letter **m** to spell my name.

I am a

____ oose!

doodle

Trace the letter **m**.
Turn it into a picture!

m

Instant Practice Packets: Alphabet • © 2011 by Joan Novelli & Holly Grundon • Scholastic Teaching Resources

Write the letter **Nn**.

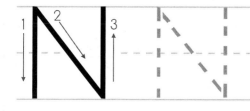

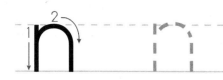

The letter **N** can look like this.   Make a new **N**.

N	N	N	

The letter **n** can look like this.   Make a new **n**.

n	n	n	

Sign It!

You can use hand shapes to make letters. Try making an **Nn**!

Name: _____ Date: _____

Write the letter **Nn**.

N

n

Letter Walk

Take a
Letter Walk.
Color each
◯ with
N or **n**.

Instant Practice Packets: Alphabet • © 2011 by Joan Novelli & Holly Grundon • Scholastic Teaching Resources

Name: _____ Date: _____ page 3

Read and Write

Nn  nest

Nn **9** ___ine

Nn

Write words with the letter **n**.
Color the ☆ for each word you know.

Animal ABCs

What am I? Write the letter **n** to spell my name.

I am a ___ ewt!

Trace the letter **n**.
Turn it into a picture!

Instant Practice Packets: Alphabet • © 2011 by Joan Novelli & Holly Grundon • Scholastic Teaching Resources

Write the letter **Oo**.

The letter **O** can look like this.   Make a new **O**.

O	O	*O*	

The letter **o** can look like this.   Make a new **o**.

o	o	*o*	

Sign It!

You can use hand shapes to make letters. Try making an **Oo**!

Write the letter **Oo**.

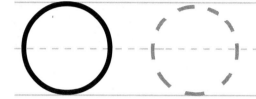

Take a
Letter Walk.
Color each
⬡ with
O or **o**.

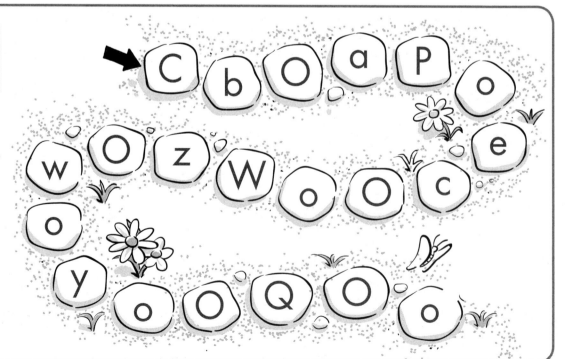

Instant Practice Packets: Alphabet • © 2011 by Joan Novelli & Holly Grundon • Scholastic Teaching Resources

Read and Write

O o octopus

___wl

Write words with the letter **o**.
Color the ☆ for each word you know.

☆  _of_

☆  _on_

☆  _out_

☆  _over_

Animal ABCs

What am I? Write the
letter **o** to spell my name.

I am an
___strich!

doodle

Trace the letter **o**.
Turn it into a picture!

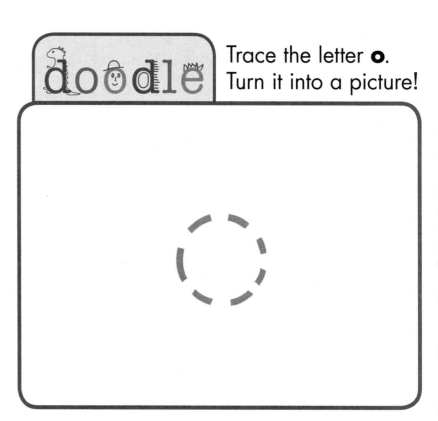

Instant Practice Packets: Alphabet • © 2011 by Joan Novelli & Holly Grundon • Scholastic Teaching Resources

Write the letter **Pp**.

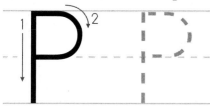

The letter **P** can look like this.   Make a new **P**.

| P | P | P | |

The letter **p** can look like this.   Make a new **p**.

| p | p | p | |

Sign It!

You can use hand shapes to make letters. Try making a **Pp**!

Name: _____ Date: _____

Write the letter **Pp**.

P P

p p

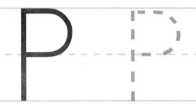

Take a
Letter Walk.
Color each
◯ with
P or **p**.

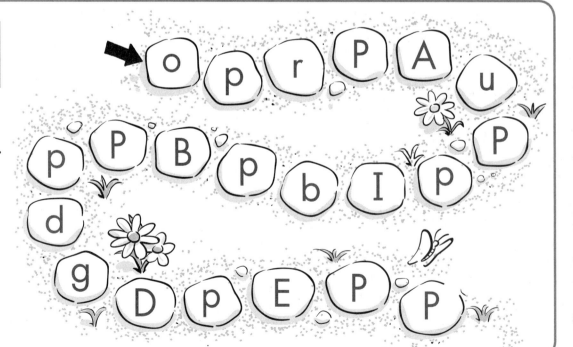

Instant Practice Packets: Alphabet • © 2011 by Joan Novelli & Holly Grundon • Scholastic Teaching Resources

Name: _____ Date: _____

Read and Write

P p  pig

P p  ____izza

P p

_____

Write words with the letter **p**.
Color the ☆ for each word you know.

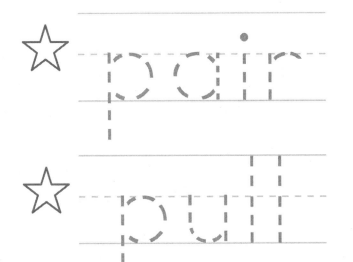

☆ pair

☆ pick

☆ pull

☆ put

Animal ABCs

What am I? Write the
letter **p** to spell my name.

I am a
___ enguin!

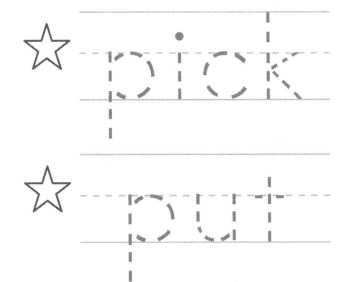

doodle

Trace the letter **p**.
Turn it into a picture!

p

74   Instant Practice Packets: Alphabet • © 2011 by Joan Novelli & Holly Grundon • Scholastic Teaching Resources

Name: _____ Date: _____

Write the letter **Qq**.

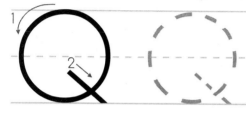

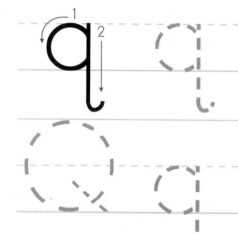

The letter **Q** can look like this. Make a new **Q**.

Q	Q	Q	

The letter **q** can look like this. Make a new **q**.

q	q	q	

Sign It!

You can use hand shapes to make letters. Try making a **Qq**!

Instant Practice Packets: Alphabet • © 2011 by Joan Novelli & Holly Grundon • Scholastic Teaching Resources

Write the letter **Qq**.

Q

q

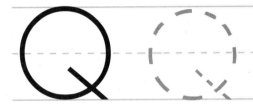

Take a
Letter Walk.
Color each
◯ with
Q or **q**.

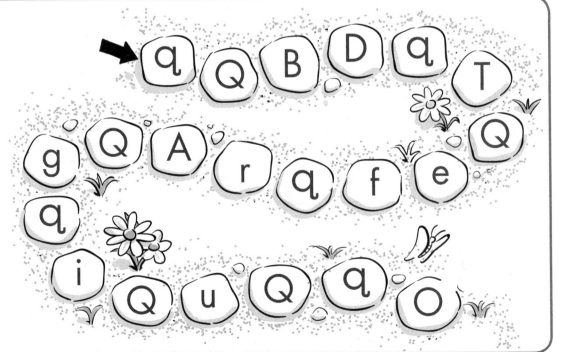

Instant Practice Packets: Alphabet • © 2011 by Joan Novelli & Holly Grundon • Scholastic Teaching Resources

Name: _____ Date: _____ page 3

Read and Write

Qq   queen

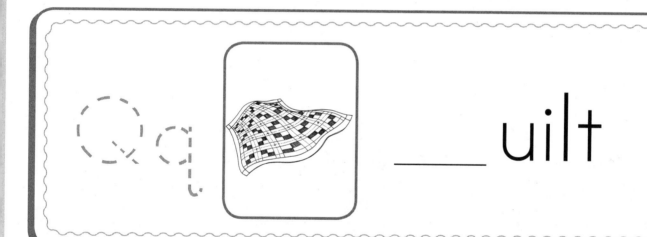

Qq   ___uilt

Qq   _____

Name: _____   Date: _____

Star Words

Write words with the letter **q**.
Color the ☆ for each word you know.

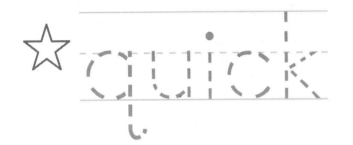

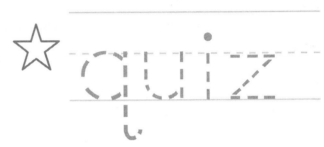

Animal ABCs

What am I? Write the
letter **q** to spell my name.

I am a
 **uail!**

doodle

Trace the letter **q**.
Turn it into a picture!

Instant Practice Packets: Alphabet • © 2011 by Joan Novelli & Holly Grundon • Scholastic Teaching Resources

Write the letter **Rr**.

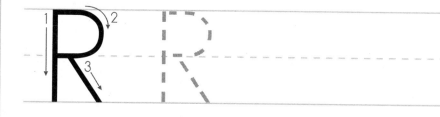

The letter **R** can look like this.   Make a new **R**.

R	R	R	

The letter **r** can look like this.   Make a new **r**.

r	r	r	

Sign It!

You can use hand shapes to make letters. Try making an **Rr**!

Instant Practice Packets: Alphabet • © 2011 by Joan Novelli & Holly Grundon • Scholastic Teaching Resources

Write the letter **Rr**.

R R

r r

Letter Walk

Take a
Letter Walk.
Color each
◯ with
R or **r**.

Read and Write

R r  ring

R r  ___obot

R r  _____

Star Words

Write words with the letter **r**.
Color the ☆ for each word you know.

Animal ABCs

What am I? Write the
letter **r** to spell my name.

I am a

____ooster!

doodle

Trace the letter **r**.
Turn it into a picture!

r

Instant Practice Packets: Alphabet • © 2011 by Joan Novelli & Holly Grundon • Scholastic Teaching Resources

Name: _____ Date: _____

Write the letter **Ss**.

The letter **S** can look like this.   Make a new **S**.

S	S	S	

The letter **s** can look like this.   Make a new **s**.

s	s	s	

Sign It!

You can use hand shapes to make letters. Try making an **Ss**!

Instant Practice Packets: Alphabet • © 2011 by Joan Novelli & Holly Grundon • Scholastic Teaching Resources

83

Name: _____ Date: _____

Write the letter **Ss**.

S   s

S   s

Take a
Letter Walk.
Color each
◯ with
S or **s**.

Instant Practice Packets: Alphabet • © 2011 by Joan Novelli & Holly Grundon • Scholastic Teaching Resources

Read and Write

S s **7** seven

S s  ___ock

S s

_____

Name: _____   Date: _____

Write words with the letter **s**.
Color the ☆ for each word you know.

☆ say

☆ see

☆ sit

☆ some

Animal ABCs

What am I? Write the letter **s** to spell my name.

I am a
___ eal!

doodle

Trace the letter **s**.
Turn it into a picture!

s

Instant Practice Packets: Alphabet • © 2011 by Joan Novelli & Holly Grundon • Scholastic Teaching Resources

Name: _____ Date: _____ page 1

Write the letter **Tt**.

The letter **T** can look like this.   Make a new **T**.

T	T	*T*	

The letter **t** can look like this.   Make a new **t**.

t	t	*t*	

Sign It!

You can use hand shapes to make letters. Try making a **Tt**!

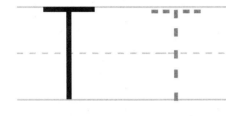

Name: _____ Date: _____ page 2

Write the letter **Tt**.

T

t

Take a
Letter Walk.
Color each
◯ with
T or **t**.

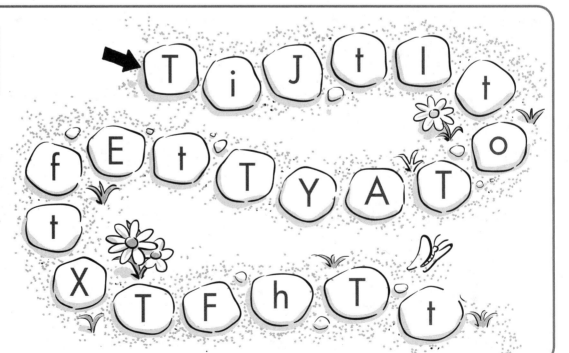

88   *Instant Practice Packets: Alphabet* • © 2011 by Joan Novelli & Holly Grundon • Scholastic Teaching Resources

Read and Write

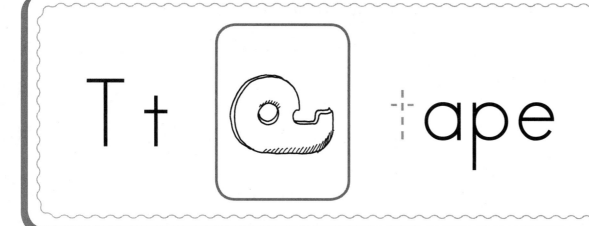

T t **tape**

T t **____iger**

T t _____

Star Words

Write words with the letter **t**.
Color the ☆ for each word you know.

☆

☆

☆

☆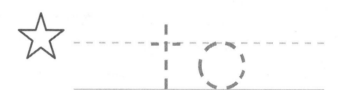

Animal ABCs

What am I? Write the letter **t** to spell my name.

I am a

___urtle!

doodle

Trace the letter **t**.
Turn it into a picture!

t

Instant Practice Packets: Alphabet • © 2011 by Joan Novelli & Holly Grundon • Scholastic Teaching Resources

Name: _____   Date: _____   page 1

Write the letter **Uu**.

The letter **U** can look like this.   Make a new **U**.

| U | u | U | |

The letter **u** can look like this.   Make a new **u**.

| u | u | *u* | |

Sign It!

You can use hand shapes to make letters. Try making a **Uu**!

Name: _____ Date: _____ page 2

Write the letter **Uu**.

U

u

Take a
Letter Walk.
Color each
○ with
U or **u**.

Instant Practice Packets: Alphabet • © 2011 by Joan Novelli & Holly Grundon • Scholastic Teaching Resources

Name: _____ Date: _____

Read and Write

U u  umbrella

U u 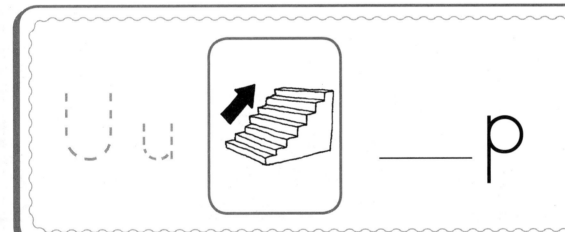 ___p

U u

_____

Star Words

Write words with the letter **u**.
Color the ☆ for each word you know.

☆

☆

☆

☆

Animal ABCs

What am I? Write the
letter **u** to spell my name.

I am a

____ nicorn!

doodle

Trace the letter **u**.
Turn it into a picture!

Instant Practice Packets: Alphabet • © 2011 by Joan Novelli & Holly Grundon • Scholastic Teaching Resources

Name: _____ Date: _____ page 1

Write the letter **Vv**.

The letter **V** can look like this.   Make a new **V**.

V	V	V	

The letter **v** can look like this.   Make a new **v**.

v	v	ν	

Sign It!

You can use hand shapes to make letters. Try making a **Vv**!

Name: _____ Date: _____

Write the letter **Vv**.

V   V

V   v

Letter Walk 👣

Take a Letter Walk. Color each ⬭ with **V** or **v**.

Instant Practice Packets: Alphabet • © 2011 by Joan Novelli & Holly Grundon • Scholastic Teaching Resources

Read and Write

V v  violin

V v  ___olcano

V v 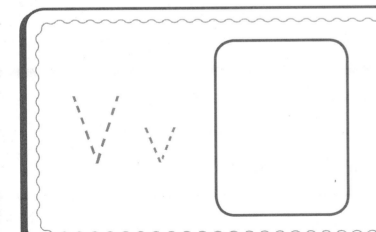 _____

Name: _____   Date: _____

Write words with the letter **v**.
Color the ☆ for each word you know.

☆ van

☆ very

☆ vest

☆ visit

Animal ABCs

What am I? Write the letter **v** to spell my name.

I am a
____ulture!

Trace the letter **v**.
Turn it into a picture!

v

Instant Practice Packets: Alphabet • © 2011 by Joan Novelli & Holly Grundon • Scholastic Teaching Resources

Name: _____ Date: _____ page 1

Write the letter **Ww**.

The letter **W** can look like this. Make a new **W**.

W	W	W	

The letter **w** can look like this. Make a new **w**.

w	ɯ	w	

Sign It!

You can use hand shapes to make letters. Try making a **Ww**!

Instant Practice Packets: Alphabet • © 2011 by Joan Novelli & Holly Grundon • Scholastic Teaching Resources

99

Name: _____   Date: _____

Write the letter **Ww**.

W W W

W W

Take a
Letter Walk.
Color each ⬡ with
W or **w**.

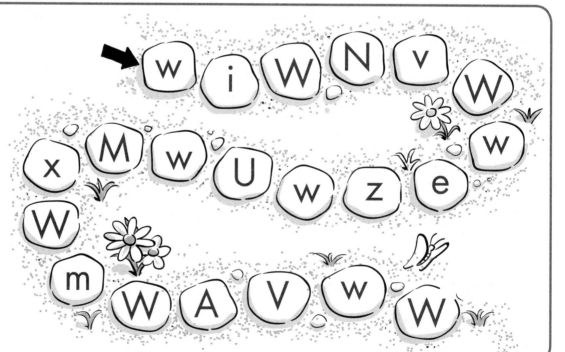

Instant Practice Packets: Alphabet • © 2011 by Joan Novelli & Holly Grundon • Scholastic Teaching Resources

Read and Write

W w wagon

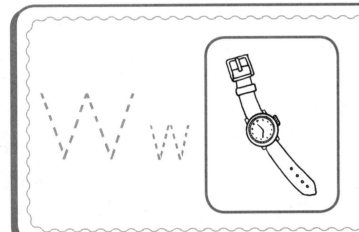

W w ___atch

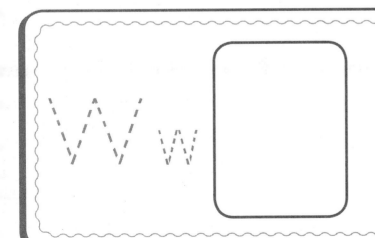

W w _____

Star Words

Write words with the letter **w**.
Color the ☆ for each word you know.

☆

☆

☆

☆

Animal ABCs

What am I? Write the letter **w** to spell my name.

I am a ___ alrus!

doodle

Trace the letter **w**.
Turn it into a picture!

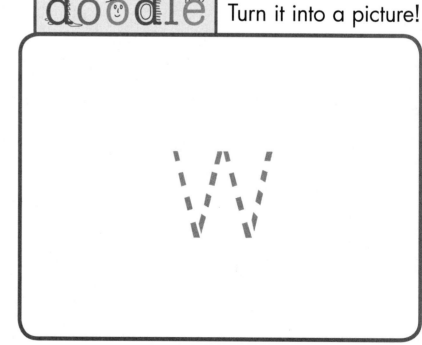

Instant Practice Packets: Alphabet • © 2011 by Joan Novelli & Holly Grundon • Scholastic Teaching Resources

Xx

ame: _____ Date: _____ page 1

Write the letter **Xx**.

The letter **X** can look like this. Make a new **X**.

X	X	X	

The letter **x** can look like this. Make a new **x**.

x	x	x	

Sign It!

You can use hand shapes to make letters. Try making an **Xx**!

Name: _____ Date: _____

Write the letter **Xx**.

X   X

x   x

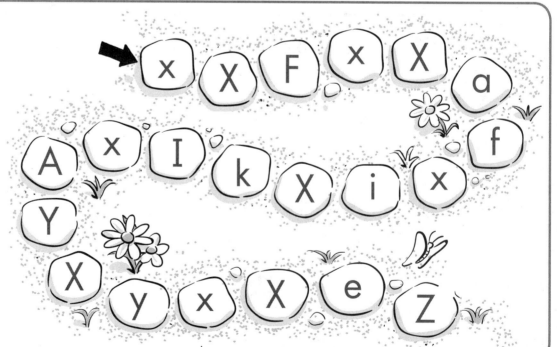

Letter Walk

Take a
Letter Walk.
Color each
⬡ with
X or **x**.

Instant Practice Packets: Alphabet • © 2011 by Joan Novelli & Holly Grundon • Scholastic Teaching Resources

Read and Write

X x   bo x

X x   o ____

X x   _____

Star Words

Write words with the letter **x**.
Color the ☆ for each word you know.

☆  ax

☆  fox

☆  mix

☆  six

Animal ABCs

What am I? Write the letter **x** to spell my name.

I am an
____-ray fish!

doodle

Trace the letter **x**.
Turn it into a picture!

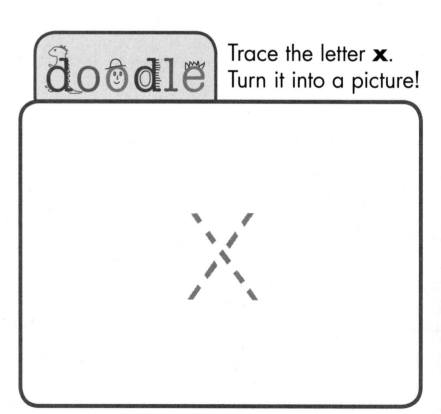

Instant Practice Packets: Alphabet • © 2011 by Joan Novelli & Holly Grundon • Scholastic Teaching Resources

Yy

Name: _____ Date: _____

Write the letter **Yy**.

Y Y

y y

The letter **Y** can look like this.   Make a new **Y**.

Y	Y	Y	

The letter **y** can look like this.   Make a new **y**.

y	y	y	

Sign It!

You can use hand shapes to make letters. Try making a **Yy**!

Name: _____   Date: _____

Write the letter **Yy**.

Y   Y

y   Y

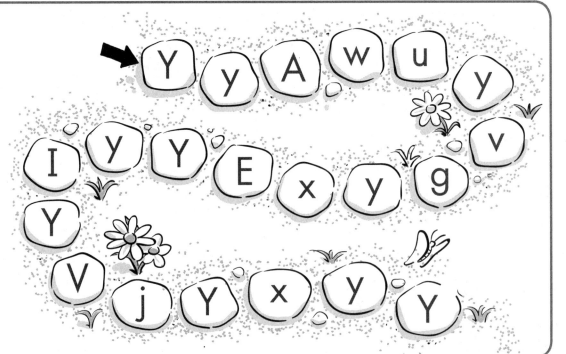

Letter Walk

Take a Letter Walk. Color each ◯ with **Y** or **y**.

Instant Practice Packets: Alphabet • © 2011 by Joan Novelli & Holly Grundon • Scholastic Teaching Resources

Name: _____ Date: _____ page 3

Read and Write

Y y   yarn

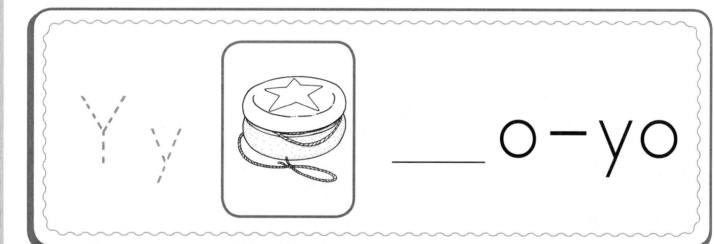

Y y   ___o-yo

Y y   _____

Name: _____ Date: _____

Star Words

Write words with the letter **y**.
Color the ☆ for each word you know.

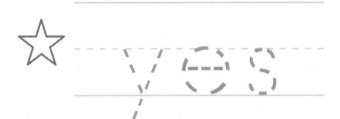

Animal ABCs

What am I? Write the letter **y** to spell my name.

I am a

___ak!

doodle

Trace the letter **y**.
Turn it into a picture!

Instant Practice Packets: Alphabet • © 2011 by Joan Novelli & Holly Grundon • Scholastic Teaching Resources

Name: _____ Date: _____ page 1

Write the letter **Zz**.

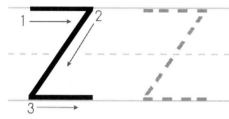

The letter **Z** can look like this.   Make a new **z**.

Z	Z	Z	

The letter **z** can look like this.   Make a new **z**.

z	z	z	

Sign It!

You can use hand shapes to make letters. Try making a **Zz**!

Write the letter **Zz**.

Z Z

z z

Letter Walk 👣

Take a Letter Walk. Color each ⬡ with **Z** or **z**.

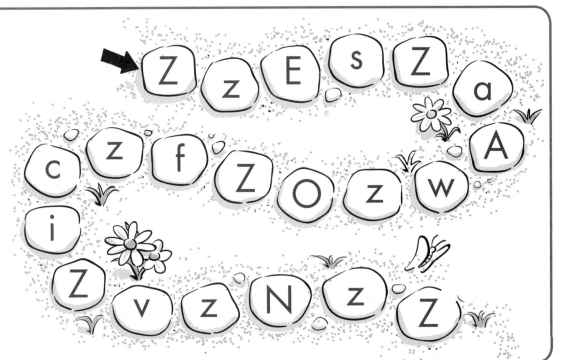

Instant Practice Packets: Alphabet • © 2011 by Joan Novelli & Holly Grundon • Scholastic Teaching Resources

Read and Write

Z z **0** zero

Z z 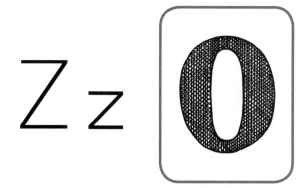 ___ip

Z z _____

Write words with the letter **z**.
Color the ☆ for each word you know.

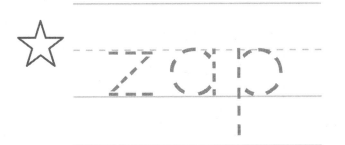

☆ zap

☆ zone

☆ zoo

☆ zoom

Animal ABCs

What am I? Write the letter **z** to spell my name.

**I am a
___ ebra!**

Trace the letter **z**.
Turn it into a picture!

z

Instant Practice Packets: Alphabet • © 2011 by Joan Novelli & Holly Grundon • Scholastic Teaching Resources

Name: _____   Date: _____

Letter Formation Practice

Letter Cards

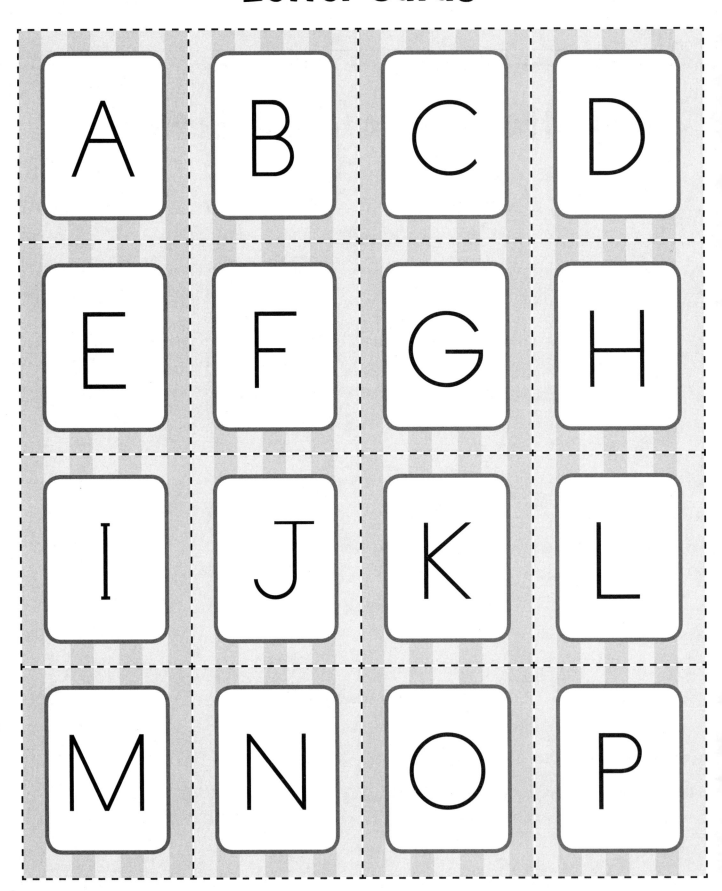

Instant Practice Packets: Alphabet • © 2011 by Joan Novelli & Holly Grundon • Scholastic Teaching Resources

Letter Cards

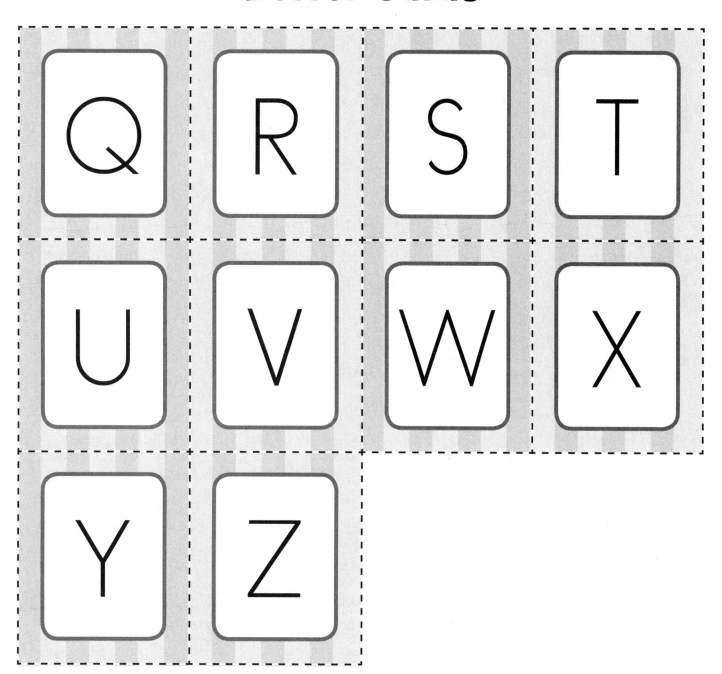

Letter Cards

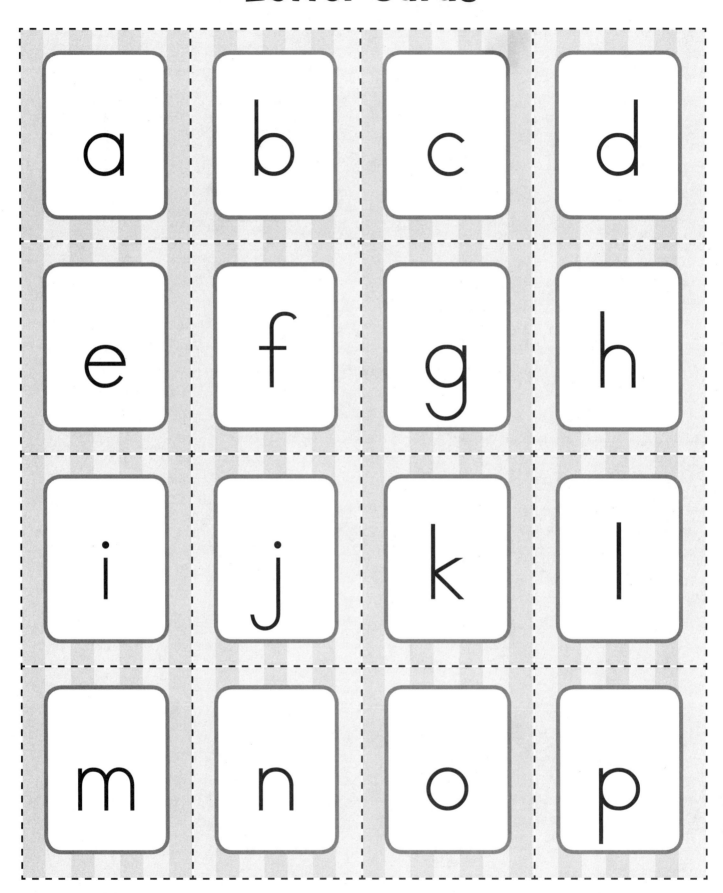

Instant Practice Packets: Alphabet • © 2011 by Joan Novelli & Holly Grundon • Scholastic Teaching Resources

Letter Cards

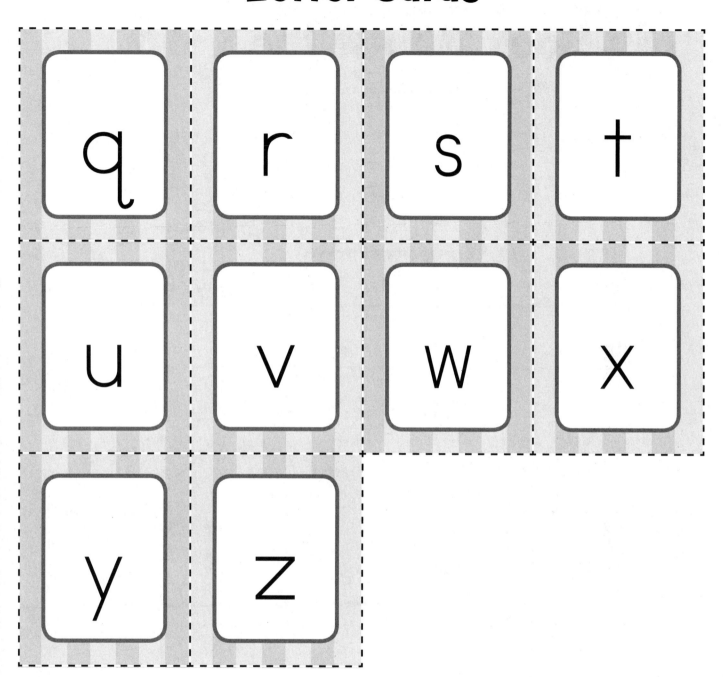

q r s t

u v w x

y z

My Book About the Letter

by

I can write the letter  !

Instant Practice-Ready Alphabet • © 2011 by Joan Novelli & Holly Grundon • Scholastic Teaching Resources (page 120)

I know what the letter [ ] looks like!

2

I can make a rainbow letter [ ] !

3

Instant Practice Packets: Alphabet • © 2011 by Joan Novelli & Holly Grundon • Scholastic Teaching Resources (page 121)

Four in a Row

I know my ABCs in order!

④

Letter Hunt

I found the letter _____ in four words.

①
②
③
④

⑤

Missing Letters GAME

Y · C · R · MOVE BACK 1 · H · M

Q · · · · · U

FREE · I · X · E · L · B

W · · Missing Letters GAME · · MOVE AHEAD 2

F · · · · · Z

N · MOVE AHEAD 1 · S · A · O · J

K · · · · · FREE

D · T · MOVE BACK 2 · V · G · P

Missing Letters GAME

b · MOVE BACK 1 · n · p · i · e

j · t

s · w · g · FREE · a · x

MOVE AHEAD 1 · k

z · MOVE AHEAD 2

d · u · MOVE BACK 2 · o · r · m

y · v

l · f · q · FREE · c · h

Instant Practice Packets: Alphabet • © 2011 by Joan Novelli & Holly Grundon • Scholastic Teaching Resources

Missing Letters Game

Materials

- Game board
- Number cube or die
- Game card
  (one per player)
- Game marker
  (one per player)
- Dry erase pen
  (one per player)
- Paper towels

How to Play

1. Choose a game marker. Place it on any "letter" space. (Players may share a space.)

2. Take turns rolling the number cube. Move that number of spaces (in any direction), then follow the directions on the space, as indicated below:

- "Letter" space: Check your game card for that letter of the alphabet. Write the letter in the correct place if it is missing.
- "Free" space: Fill in any one missing letter on your game card.
- "Move ahead…" or "Move back…" space: Move as directed and check your game card for that letter. Write the letter, if it is missing.

3. Keep playing until one player fills in all missing letters on his or her game card (or play until all players complete their cards). Erase your game card and play again.

Missing Letters 1

A B __ D __ F G __ __ J

K L __ N __ P __ R __ T

U __ W X __ Z

Missing Letters Game Cards

Missing Letters 2

A __ C __ E F __ H I __

__ L M __ O __ Q R S __

U V __ X Y __

Missing Letters 3

__ b __ d __ f g __ i j

__ __ m n __ p __ r s __

u v w __ y z

Instant Practice Packets: Alphabet • © 2011 by Joan Novelli & Holly Grundon • Scholastic Teaching Resources

Missing Letters Game Cards

Missing Letters **4**

a __ c __ e __ g h i __

k l __ n o __ q __ s __

u v w __ y __

Missing Letters

___ ___ ___ ___ ___ ___ ___ ___ ___

___ ___ ___ ___ ___ ___ ___ ___

___ ___ ___ ___ ___ ___ ___ ___

Alphabet Hand Signs

Aa Bb Cc

Dd Ee Ff Gg Hh

Ii Jj Kk Ll Mm

Nn Oo Pp Qq Rr

Ss Tt Uu Vv Ww

Xx Yy Zz

Instant Practice Packets: Alphabet • © 2011 by Joan Novelli & Holly Grundon • Scholastic Teaching Resources